Dr. Gwen's
A to Z Self-Care Guide for Educators

Practical Tips, Tools and Strategies

Gwendolyn A. Martin, Ed.D., LPC

Dedication

This book is dedicated to every educator who aspires to make SELF-CARE a priority!

Also by Dr. Gwen

Make Yourself A Priority (Journal)

My Message to Educators

The role and responsibility of educators continue to increase, causing professionals to experience feelings of being overwhelmed, anxious, and stressed. The code of Ethics for the American Counseling Association (ACA, 2014) states that counselors should "engage in self-care activities" to maintain and promote emotional, physical, mental, and spiritual well-being to best meet professional obligations." Similarly, The Code of Ethics for the Association of American Educators states that professional educators should "maintain sound mental health." Self-care is not just a personal matter. It is an ethical responsibility. We have a moral obligation to not only care for others but to care for ourselves too. The message is clear. You give the best care to your clients when you take sufficient care of yourself.

Self-care begins with self-awareness and prioritizing the value of you as a person. While you are on this self-care journey, it is imperative that you make yourself a priority. Many of us are guilty of giving more time, energy, and attention to the profession than our family, friends, and more importantly, ourselves. We lack self-empathy and do not take the time or space needed to care for ourselves without feeling selfish, guilty, or needy. We must learn to give ourselves the same love and attention we freely give others daily. Our needs matter too! Today is the day to start taking the time to do things that make you happy and make you feel loved, fulfilled, and appreciated. Every day is a new opportunity to show up, show out, and show yourself that you are worthy. Challenge yourself and make every day count. Always bet on YOU! I am rooting for you 100%.

Introduction

I am excited to share Dr. Gwen's A to Z Self-Care Guide for Educators, a blend of inspiration, motivation, education, and simple, practical solutions that can easily be incorporated into your existing daily routine. Self-care is all about engaging in activities and practices on a regular basis to reduce stress and preserve or enhance your overall health and well-being. Counselors, educators, and those of us in helping professions are good at attending to the well-being of others while neglecting our own needs – until it is too late and we are overwhelmed, exhausted, sick, or burnt out. Small changes and active engagement in even basic self-care routines have significant health benefits. Little changes can help you reduce stress and anxiety, improve your mental health, prevent illness, achieve optimal results, and make your dreams a reality.

Many educators are struggling and feeling stressed, unappreciated, and unhappy. Some of you may be nearing burnout, suffering from secondary trauma, or compassion fatigue (yes, the struggle is real!). We are not living the healthy, connected, purpose-driven lives we are capable of, desire, and deserve. We are so busy with endless to-do-lists that we are sacrificing our health, families, goals, and dreams. It is time to start taking better care of ourselves. We need to practice self-care in every aspect of our lives to include school, work, and home, so that we can get healthy, be more effective, efficient, and ultimately live our best lives.

Never-ending responsibilities (mom/dad, wife/husband son/daughter, teacher, counselor, administrator, coach, caretaker, student etc.) and our very hectic lives make it is easy to forget that self-care is essential, necessary, and non-negotiable. It is the thing we MUST do. We need to make sure that we are taking care while giving care to others. Let's not forget about our needs. We are more than just an educator or counselor there to help others. We are a people too, with our own interests, needs, and desires. Whether our passion is painting, gardening, pottery, sports, cooking etc., we must make sure that we take time to do what we love. Although the work we do is important, our job should not be the center of our lives. We should make time regularly to do something we really love to do that does not involve work (weekly or daily if possible). This is an investment in YOU! Now is the time to start taking better care of SELF by making yourself a priority. Start today!

We have a professional, personal, and moral responsibility to maintain a healthy and balanced lifestyle at home and work. This book is a guide to help educators reduce stress, restore health, and reach personal and professional goals and dreams. It incorporates proactive activities, healthy practices, and specific routines that can be customized to fit individual needs. I suggest that you read the book and incorporate strategies that are meaningful to you. This book is packed with information that will inspire you to act NOW.

I envision Dr. Gwen's A to Z Self-Care Guide, being read, first, by beginning and seasoned educators (administrators, teachers, counselors, aides etc.) and other professions (social workers, healthcare workers) who seek guidance on making self-care a priority in their daily lives. Second, I envision this guide as a suggested reading in education and counseling courses. The book will fit easily into ethics and professional preparation courses. Third, this book will be a great resource to provide new staff during orientations. Let's give individuals new to the profession tools they can use to start them off on the right track, thereby setting them up for success. Finally, this guide may be used during professional development workshops and trainings to highlight the importance of caring for SELF.

I pray, by learning to incorporate daily self-care strategies, as educators, we become healthier and happier in every aspect of our lives. We will maximize our potential in all areas of self-care – physical, emotional, psychological, spiritual, and professional – giving us the strength, energy, motivation, and support to live life to the fullest.

Focus on making small improvements. Each change you make moves you closer to optimal health and well-being. Included are Dr. Gwen's Self-Care Tips throughout the book to help. Practice these tips, tools, and strategies and share them with your family, friends, colleagues, and community.

Let us support each other on this self-care journey to better health and wellness.

Peace and Blessings,

Dr. Gwen

SELF

Change your mindset and attitude.

Ask for help when needed.

Rest, release, recharge, and renew.

Eat healthy and exercise regularly.

Self-Care Love Letter

TODAY IS THE DAY!

Today is a new beginning. You have decided to make self-care a priority in your life. As you embark on this journey, take some time to assess where you are at this moment and where you would like to be (your dream come true) by writing a Self-Care Love Letter to yourself. Because you are motivated, inspired, and committed to being healthy and happy, several pages are dedicated solely to this purpose.

While writing this Self-Care Love Letter, take time to pause, reflect, express gratitude, and show appreciation for who you are, and set future goals (big and small) that will bring you closer to realizing your dream life. This letter will give your life purpose, set a clear vision of what you want to achieve, and help you create an action plan.

Writing a Self-Care Love Letter is empowering. It will improve your mood, reduce stress and anxiety, provide accountability, and increase your likelihood of success. As you begin writing, take a moment to reflect on why you decided NOW is the time to make changes in your life. Be open, transparent, and nonjudgmental of your feelings, ideas, hopes, and dreams as they surface. Get it all out – release and let go! After completing this guide, as you continue your self-care journey, look back and reflect on the progression…challenges, and triumphs.

Google the link below and listen to the audio letters I wrote just for me, but I am openly sharing them with you. They were written six months apart.

https://screencast-o-matic.com/watch/crnI2fSus8

My Self-Care Love Letter

_____

_____

_____

_____

_____

_____

_____

_____

_____

_____

_____

_____

_____

_____

_____

_____

A

Asking for help is not a sign of weakness. It takes great insight to know what you need and courage to ask for it.

A – Ask for help and feedback.

Asking for help is a hard thing for many of us to do. However, asking for help is a healthy natural response to challenging situations. You should not be working in isolation. You do not have to struggle with difficult situations on your own. As teachers, counselors, helpers, women, and men, we cannot be all-knowing and doing (although we feel like that is the expectation at times). Seek help, consultation, support, and ideas from colleagues, supervisors, mentors, and others in your community. One person cannot handle the needs of everyone, but collectively as counselors, teachers, principals, nurses, etc., we can find solutions. As educators, we must practice what we preach. We must model for our students and colleagues that asking for help is okay. It is not a sign of weakness or inadequacy. It takes a lot of insight and strength to know what you need and courage to ask for it. As the saying goes, "teamwork makes the dreamwork." Collaboration and consultation can make a world of difference.

Psst.... Asking for help and feedback at home is a good self-care practice too. Let your family and friends pitch in and help.

Dr. Gwen's Self-Care Tip

Make a list of people you can ask for help and call on for support.

Family:

Friends:

Colleagues:

Spiritual Leaders:

Mentors:

Coaches:

Community Leaders:

Counselors:

When asking for help, be direct and specific about what you need. Communicate what you have done to try to solve the problem yourself first. People are more apt to help you if they know that you are trying to help yourself.

Examples:

Will you please show me how to upload this file? I have tried, but I keep getting this error message that says the file cannot be uploaded.

Do you know where I can find _____? I have done a Google Search, looked through curriculum materials online and in the office but have not been able to locate it.

My son/daughter is struggling in math, especially with this remote learning. I help as much as possible, but math is not my thing. Would you be willing to help him/her or know of any resources that we can use when we get stuck?

Will you please let me know if you hear about any food drives or organizations that assist needy families in the area? My family could use the support right now.

I am trying to cut meat out of my diet, and I am not the best cook. I am struggling to come up with recipes. I know you love to cook and have great recipe ideas. Do you mind sharing some with me?

I got stuck in a meeting after work and forgot to take something out for dinner. Do you mind picking up something on the way home?

B

Breathe life back into:

Your Ambitions

Your Desires

Your Goals

and

Your Relationships.

B – Breathe (do 5-5-5).

Deep breathing is a simple, convenient way to alleviate stress and anxiety, reduce pain, high blood pressure, and aids in digestion. When your emotions are in motion (frustration, anger, nervousness, anxiety, sadness), try taking deep breaths to help you calm down.

Follow these four steps to give 5-5-5 breathing a try.

1. Slowly take a big breath in (inhale) for 5 seconds: 1-2-3-4-5
   Breathe in slowly and calmly, through the nose, filling your abdomen and chest. Pretend you are smelling a large bouquet of flowers or some yummy baked goods.

2. Hold this breathe in for 5 seconds: 1-2-3-4-5

3. Slowly release your breath (exhale) for 5 seconds: 1-2-3-4-5
   Breathe out through a slightly parted lip or "O" shaped lips. Pretend you are blowing out the candles on a birthday cake, or you are trying to blow a big bubble without popping it.

4. Repeat the process 3-4 more times.

You should begin to feel yourself start to calm down. You are now ready to re-engage.

Dr. Gwen's Self-Care Tip

Make it a daily practice to stop several times throughout the day and JUST BREATHE!

Start first thing in the morning during meditation, take a few minutes during lunch to give your brain a break, and then again at night before bed to help you relax and prepare your body for sleep.

Creatively find ways to consistently incorporate deep breathing into your daily schedule.

1. Place a post-it note on your bathroom mirror as a reminder to start the day with a few deep breaths while in the shower or getting dressed for work.

2. Take a few moments to do some deep breathing when you first arrive at work to start the day in a calm state.

3. The drive home from work may be an optimal time to release all the weight of the day.

In the beginning, it might be helpful to schedule reminders on your phone until it becomes a normal part of your daily routine.

Sometimes the most important thing we do all day is rest between two deep breaths.

Stop and put things in perspective.

INHALE peace and EXHALE stress.

C

Focus on the things you can change.

Your Attitude

Your Mindset

Your Energy.

C – Change your mindset and attitude.

You have the power to change the way you look at things. Regardless of your current situation, how you think (mindset) and react (attitude) is truly 100% up to you. When we change our thinking, actions, and willingness to learn, the potential for greatness becomes limitless. Psychologist Dr. Carol Dweck's research has proven that we must change our mindset from fixed to growth. A fixed mindset is a belief that our intelligence and our talents are innate and set, so we avoid challenges and easily give up when we encounter setbacks. A growth mindset, on the other hand, believes that intelligence and talents can be developed through hard work, good strategies, and input from others. Having a growth mindset increases our motivation, abilities, and achievements. We are more apt to take on challenges and learn and grow from them. Choose a positive outlook, choose happy thoughts, and keep on learning and growing.

Dr. Gwen's Self-Care Tip

Just like self-care is a journey, creating a growth mindset is too. One of my favorite quotes by Dr. Dweck is, *"The path to a growth mindset is a journey, not a proclamation."* Here are three mindset activities to use as you start the journey to becoming more growth-minded and aligned with the person you want to be. This is just the beginning.

1. **Ask for help when needed. (Refer back to letter A.)**

   If you are struggling in any area of your life, having a growth mindset is essential for improvement. Whether it is pursuing professional goals, getting healthy, learning a new skill, or being a better life partner, having a growth mindset is advantageous. Sometimes you need someone more skilled (mentor, coach, counselor) to lead, guide, and support you. Do not waste time floundering. Reach out and ask someone for help.

2. **Use failure as an opportunity for improvement. (See letter F.)**

   When you fail at something, ask yourself what worked, what did not work, and what you could have done differently. Learn new strategies to overcome obstacles. As educators, we are notorious for working harder instead of smarter. We often invest more time doing the same thing with the hope of improving the next time instead of changing what we do.

I have a perfect example. A few years ago, I worked closely with a group of exceptional teachers who were frustrated with their stagnate test scores. After analyzing the results, I realized that they were wasting time teaching skills that were not even assessed on the test while neglecting to teach many skills the students were expected to know. We made a few changes, and teachers saw a remarkable improvement the next year.

3. **Learn the power of "Yet".**

Instead of saying I do not know how to do something, try saying I do not know how to do that "yet." It is a concept that educators try to teach children daily, but as adults, we need to be mindful of this opportunity for growth too. YET is a powerful word because it leaves the door open to broadening our personal and professional development. You have not YET reached your full potential. That's inspiring!

A good way to determine where you are on the mindset continuum (fixed – mixed – growth) is to take an assessment. Mindsetworks.com has a short mindset assessment that gives you immediate results and feedback.

D

Daily devotion is better than yearly resolution.

D – Daily Devotion.

You probably thought this section was going to be spiritual. Nope! That is covered in other parts of the book. This section is about daily devotion that entails making small, consistent steps each day that gets you closer and closer to realizing your dreams. I believe that dreams and daily devotion can help you achieve anything in life. When you put effort into something every single day, that's when transformation happens. That is how change occurs. Set your goals and take action.

Dreams are immensely powerful. They are our innermost, cherished hopes and aspirations. Dreams inspire, motivate, and help us overcome challenges and obstacles. They have the power to transform our lives for the better.

Dr. Gwen's Self-Care Tip

DREAM BIG! Put aside all your doubts and fears of failure and just dream. Do not let your thoughts or the thoughts and beliefs of other people constrain you. Free up your mind and think about all the infinite possibilities in life. Stop worrying about all the things that could go wrong and focus on what your life will be like when your dreams come true. Nothing is impossible. Act NOW!

Here are 15 of my favorite dream quotes to inspire you.

1. First, think. Second, believe. Third, dream. And finally, dare. ~ Walt Disney

2. All our dreams can come true if we have the courage to pursue them. ~ Walt Disney

3. Dare to live the life you have dreamed for yourself. Go forward and make your dreams come true. ~ Ralph Waldo Emerson

4. If you don't build your dreams, someone will hire you to help build theirs. ~ Tony Gaskin

5. Step away from the couch sitters who are awaiting the single perfect day to begin living their dream. You can choose to live your dream every day if you just take the first step. ~T. D. Jakes

6. You don't have to see the whole staircase, just take the first step. ~ Martin Luther King, Jr. (I would be remiss if I did not mention Dr. King's famous "I Have A Dream" speech.)

7. Amateurs sit and wait for inspiration, the rest of us just get up and go to work. ~ Stephen King

8. It always seems impossible until it's done. ~ Nelson Mandela

9. The only limit to the height of your achievements is the reach of your dreams and the willingness to work hard for them. ~ Michelle Obama

10. A dream doesn't become reality through magic; it takes sweat, determination, and hard work. ~ Colin Powell

11. So many of our dreams at first seem impossible, then they seem improbable, and then, when we summon the will, they soon become inevitable. ~ Christopher Reeve

12. The future belongs to those who believe in the beauty of their dreams. ~ Eleanor Roosevelt

13. Every great dream begins with a dreamer. Always remember, you have within you the strength, the patience, and the passion to reach for the stars to change the world. ~ Harriet Tubman

14. The biggest adventure you can take is to live the life of your dreams. ~ Oprah Winfrey

15. The key to realizing a dream is to focus not on success but significance – and then even the small steps and little victories along your path will take on greater meaning. ~ Oprah Winfrey

Hopefully at least one of these quotes resonated with you. Now it is time to put some dreams on paper. Research shows that writing down what you want to achieve significantly increases your chances of success. If you tell someone about your dream it increases the success rate even more. It adds a layer of accountability. Now let's write down the BIG Dream YOU want to achieve and some smaller ones too. Keep in mind that your big dream could be running a marathon while someone else's could be to complete a 5 km race. It does not matter how big or small your dream is if it adds value to your life. Once you have your dreams down, don't forget to tell somebody, and get to work.

Big Dream

_____

_____

_____

_____

_____

Small Dreams

_____

_____

_____

_____

_____

_____

_____

E

Being fit and healthy is 80% nutrition and 20% exercise. EAT better and EXERCISE more.

E – Eat healthy and exercise regularly

It is better to proactively prevent poor health rather than cure poor health. Eating well and exercising are essential to healthy living. We have all heard the sayings *"Eat the Rainbow"* and *"You are what you eat"*. True statements. Poor nutrition can lead to several chronic diseases such as obesity, type 2 diabetes, various cancers, Alzheimer's, and cardiovascular disease. The good news is eating a balanced diet with proper nutrition can improve your health, concentration, problem-solving, help you deal with stress, and combat diseases. A healthy diet includes fruit, vegetables, legumes (e.g., lentils and beans), nuts and whole grains (unprocessed), unsaturated fats (found in fish, avocado and nuts, and in sunflower, soybean, canola, and olive oils), low sugar and low salt intake. The World Health Organization reports that unhealthy diets and a lack of physical activity are leading global risks to health.

Research shows that exercise improves brain function and facilitates learning, creativity, and problem-solving. Physical exercise ranks among the top ways to prevent burnout. According to the American Heart Association at least 150 minutes (2.5 hours) of heart-pumping physical activity per week can help you think, feel, and sleep better as well as perform daily tasks more efficiently. Additional benefits can be gained from being active at least 300 minutes (5 hours) per week. The World Health Organization reports that people who are insufficiently active have a 20% to 30% increased risk of death compared to people who are sufficiently active. Up to 5 million deaths a year could be averted if the global population were more active.

No worries, your physical activity does not have to be running a marathon; it can be something as easy as a daily walk after dinner or during lunch. Walking can easily be incorporated into your daily life, and it is FREE. No gym membership or exercise equipment is required. Try to find ways to incorporate movement into your life. Movement is important.

As always, check with your physician or certified fitness professional before starting any exercise program.

Dr. Gwen's Self-Care Tip

The following ten strategies can get you started, get you back on track or help you maintain:

1. Eat plenty of fruits and vegetables. They are full of vitamins, minerals, dietary fiber, plant protein, and antioxidants.
2. Choose fresh fruits instead of sweet snacks such as candy, cookies, and cakes to reduce the consumption of sugars.
3. Limit your intake of high sugar drinks (soda, fruit juices, syrups, flavored milk, and yogurt drinks) to reduce your sugar intake. Drinking good ole water is the best option.
4. Limit the amount of salt and high-sodium condiments (soy sauce, marinades) when cooking and preparing foods to reduce your salt intake. Think "spices" not "sauces" when preparing food. Recipes with curry, turmeric, basil, and tarragon, for example, are flavorful—and you can use nonfat yogurt as a base.
5. Consider Intermittent fasting (IF). IF is an eating strategy where you eat for a period and fast for a period. For example, a 16:8 ratio involves 16 hours of fasting combined with an 8-hour window for eating. Combining exercise during the 16-hour fasting period helps to transform your body's physiology.
6. Reserve time in your schedule to eat a healthy lunch EVERYDAY! It is easy to skip lunch when we are busy at work. Don't do it! Pack a healthy lunch and snacks for work. This gives you control over what you eat and minimizes the chance you will opt for the snack machine.
7. Eat dinner at least two hours before bedtime.
8. Take a nature walk. Exercising in nature provides the opportunity to engage all your senses and has additional health benefits. Enjoy the sights, sounds, smells, and textures found in nature. It can improve your mood and make you feel happier and more energetic.
9. Cook healthy meals. If cooking is not your thing, buy a healthy-recipe book. Use search engines like Google or Pinterest for creativity. You could also join a healthy cooking group on Facebook. There are tons of ideas out there.
10. Skip seconds. Challenge yourself to stick to one serving (standard portion sizes) to keep your calorie intake in check.

F

Failure is a part of success. Fail until you succeed.

F – Failure is an opportunity for improvement.

Is the fear of failure keeping you from accomplishing your goals and realizing your dreams? Fear of failure can be debilitating. We need to stop viewing failure as a measure of our worth and instead view it as information and feedback that can help us grow and improve. We must move away from the mindset that says failure is embarrassing, a sign of weakness, or an indication that we are not competent. Successful people view failure as growth opportunities. They are transparent and open to sharing that they got it wrong many times before finally getting it right. They share how they capitalized on their failures and did not give up when they encountered roadblocks and setbacks. Failure is essential to learning and growth. As educators, we are in positions of influence. We need to model positive responses to failure and create environments where students and clients feel safe to explore and take risks. We should foster growth in ourselves and others.

Dr. Gwen's Self-Care Tip:

Questions to consider after a failure:

1. What part was satisfactory or really worked.

_____

_____

_____

_____

2. What went completely wrong or haywire?

_____

_____

_____

_____

3. What improvements can be made for the next time?

_____

_____

_____

4. Who can help me or support me in this effort?

_____

_____

_____

5. What timeline do I need to set to try again?

_____

_____

_____

G

Gratitude is the healthiest of all human emotions. The more you express gratitude for what you have, the more likely you will have even more to express gratitude for.

~ Zig Ziglar

G – Gratitude

Gratitude is one of the highest forms of positive energy. It is the appreciation or thankfulness for what you have, big or small, tangible, or intangible. Even on our seemingly worst days, there is always something to be grateful for... a smile, a thank you, a call from a friend, etc. Do not take these things for granted. In essence, acknowledge the goodness in your life. Make a conscious effort to count your blessings and give thanks daily. By developing an attitude of gratitude, you will open the door to new relationships personally and professionally, be happier, and improve your overall health and well-being. Studies have found that gratitude reduces mental-health disorders such as depression, anxiety, and post-traumatic stress disorder (PTSD). Studies have also found that people who show gratitude are more motivated, confident, optimistic, compassionate, and successful.

Dr. Gwen's Self-Care Tip:

Just five minutes a day spent expressing gratitude can change your life. Here are 5 simple things that you can do to express gratitude daily:

1. Write in a gratitude journal daily to focus on the positives in your life.

2. Tell someone how much you love and appreciate them and how something they did made a difference for you.

3. Compliment someone on their appearance, attire, performance, character trait or service. It will make them feel good and hopefully be a contagion.

4. Spend time being one with nature and plant seeds of happiness.

5. Volunteer or donate your time, ideas, energy, and financial contributions to an organization that helps others.

H

Sometimes we just need a hug, so we know we matter too! YES, a virtual hug will do.

H – Hug Someone.

Who does not need a hug every now and then? Stop for a minute and think of a person that gives the best hugs. You know the kind I am talking about…. warm, inviting, soothing, protective, reassuring, comforting, calming, uplifting, and stress-reducing. Hugging is often how we greet someone we love and care about and how we say goodbye. Hugs are also a celebratory response. Think about graduations, weddings, births, and holidays. I am sure that you will find yourself reflecting on some of your best memories packed full of good old-fashioned hugs.

Many studies had been conducted about a hug's remarkable healing power. Hugging is a very communicative type of touch. According to an article published by NBC News, the context of the relationship (romantic, familial, or platonic) does not matter. A simple 20-second hug is said to have medical healing properties. Hugs provide mental and physical health benefits. It can reduce stress, relieve emotions such as sadness and fear, ward off illness such as a common cold, and heal old wounds. Huggers tend to be healthier and happier people.

So, the next time one of your family, friends, colleagues, or perhaps even a stranger is stressed or in pain, go ahead and offer them a hug. If you are the person in need, it is okay to ask for a hug. A little squeeze may be just what is needed to feel better. Wouldn't it be great if we could just hug out all our problems?

Dr. Gwen's Self-Care Tip:

Here are some "VIRTUAL" hug suggestions to reach out or acknowledge someone who supported or impacted your life (no matter how small the manner). Virtual hugs are ideal when you cannot express your feelings in person. Yeah, the physical act is better, but the emotional message expressed virtually is impactful too. It says you matter.

- Handwritten note

- Old-fashioned letter (if you have a lot to say)

- Email

- Text message

- Phone Call

- Card (Hallmark or Ecard)

- GIF (Graphic Interchange Format), Emoji or Meme

- Flowers

You can also use the same means above to encourage someone.

- A student struggling in school.

- A care-provider with a sick parent or relative.

- A person suffering from a major illness.

- A person dealing with relationship issues.

- A person who has lost a job.

- A person dealing with death of a loved one.

Reaching out (even from a distance) to help and support others benefits you too. Giving has a way of touching and uniting hearts and souls.

I

There is no quick fix.

Take the time.

Invest in yourself.

YOU are worth it!

I – Invest in you, mind, body, and spirit.

Self-care is about doing what makes you feel good – mind, body, and spirit. Just like you should say NO to more things you do not want to do, you should say YES more to the things that make you smile, your soul happy, and gets you closer to achieving your dreams. Do not let the fear of failure or comfortability keep you in a box. Go ahead, enroll in that graduate program. You can do it! Accept that management position. You are good enough. Apply for that job. You are qualified and will be an asset to the organization. Indulge your urge to go to that new restaurant, party of one! Take that solo vacation. Make a commitment to invest in YOU by dedicating time and energy to your personal development.

Dr. Gwen's Self-Care Tip:

It is important to maintain a healthy balance between your mind, body, and soul. Routinely practice self-care to include your physical, mental, emotional, professional, and spiritual needs.

Here are 20 simple ways to begin investing in YOU ~ mind, body, and spirit.

1. Get regular medical check-ups.

2. Cook healthy meals.

3. Get 7–8 hours of sleep.

4. Exercise.

5. Take brain breaks.

6. Read books that challenge your mind and inspire creativity.

7. Start that business or side hustle.

8. Hire a business or career coach.

9. Forgive.

10. Meditate.

11. Express gratitude.

12. Learn a new hobby or skill.

13. Surround yourself with positive, loving, supportive people.

15. Explore other cultures (museums, travel, music).

16. Treat yourself (massage, pedicure, manicure, facial).

17. Listen to podcasts about empowering people.

18. Save and invest your money.

19. Attend a workshop or conference.

20. Apply the strategies in this book.

Write down three to five strategies you will start incorporating in your daily life because you see value, purpose, and benefits in doing so.

1. _____

_____

_____

_____

2. _____

_____

_____

3. _____

_____

4. _____

_____

_____

_____

5. _____

_____

_____

_____

Investing in yourself is the best investment you will ever make. It will not only improve your life, it will improve the lives of all those around you.

~ Robin Sharma

J

Journaling is a good way to

Pause

Reflect

and

BECOME.

Dream on!

J – Journal (Gratitude, Reflection, Mood, Drawing).

One of the ways I invest in myself daily is by journaling. It helps me train my thoughts, prioritize problems, fears, concerns, and set goals in a judgment-free zone. I am more focused when I get my thoughts and feelings out of my head and on paper. It brings clarity to my thoughts, feelings, and aspirations. It makes me feel more in control. Journaling also helps me stop, self-reflect, and provides an emotional space to express love, gratitude, and compassion. Looking back, I can see how much I have grown and changed for the better.

Journaling is an effective strategy to bring about awareness, get in touch with your feelings, gain perspective, and make connections between your motives and actions. Writing encourages you to reflect on your views and process your experiences.

Dr. Gwen's Self-Care Tip:

You may also engage your emotions by experiencing and acknowledging them in other ways. When you are frustrated with a spouse, family member, coworker, write in an "emotional journal" to get your feelings out. You may or may not share your frustration with them after you have had an opportunity to calm down. You might be surprised that the simple act of journaling can be very cathartic.

Start your daily journal entries:

I was grateful today for

_____

_____

_____

_____

_____

I was inspired

_____

_____

_____

_____

_____

I was able to smile about

_____

_____

_____

_____

_____

People who touched my life today

_____

_____

_____

_____

Something new I learned today

_____

_____

_____

_____

_____

Today I feel

_____

_____

_____

_____

_____

Tomorrow I look forward to

_____

_____

_____

_____

_____

K

KNOWLEDGE is great,

how you use it IS POWER.

K – Knowledge is POWER!

We have all heard the saying, "when you KNOW better, do better." Do not continue to make the same mistakes that got you in your current situation. Here is a quote by Kofi Annan, *"Knowledge is power. Information is liberating. Education is the premise of progress, in every society, in every family."* Indeed, knowledge is power. In essence, knowledge helps us learn from past mistakes. Just think of the knowledge you have gained so far from reading and completing the activities in this guide. Hopefully, you have already started to apply what you have learned to make changes on your journey to better health and wellness. The more knowledge you gain, the better equipped you will be to overcome any challenges and setbacks you encounter. Instead of giving up or quitting as you have in the past, you will adjust, take detours, and make better choices armed with newly acquired knowledge. Now it is time to take action.

Dr. Gwen's Self-Care Tip

Expand your knowledge base to help you accomplish your personal and professional goals and dreams. Here are a few things you can do:

1. Ask questions.
2. Attend a conference or workshop.
3. Consult and collaborate with others.
4. Hire a coach.
5. Join a group.
6. Learn a new skill or hobby.
7. READ.
8. Take a course.
9. Travel.
10. Volunteer in your community.

L

Once you stop learning,

you start dying.

~ *Albert Einstein*

L – Learn a new skill or hobby.

Learning something new at any age is powerful and can spark new cognitive abilities. The mental component of an effective self-care routine addresses your emotional needs, allows you to engage your creativity, and challenges your brain. In a creative state, our mind is open to new ideas, curious about possibilities, and willing to take spontaneous risks. Release your inner child. That is one of my favorite sayings. It is probably because I am a big kid at heart. It simply means to be free creatively and to have fun doing it whether you are good at it or not. The brain benefits from having to learn new things. Regularly challenging your brain with activities such as board games that require mental strategies, crossword puzzles, and jigsaw puzzles may help improve the lifespan of your brain cells. Physical activities and social engagements such as learning a sport (tennis, golf), learning a new dance (cha-cha, the rumba), taking a class on pottery, jewelry making, or gardening are also effective ways to keep the brain active.

Dr. Gwen's Self-Care Tip:

I have a coworker whose daughter taught herself how to sew by watching YouTube videos. The possibilities are endless in this technology-rich world. There is unlimited access to information and training at our fingertips. No excuses!

Create a list of 3 things that you want to learn to do and DO IT. But do not stop there. Keep learning and growing.

1.

2.

3.

Here are 20 ideas to get you started. What are you passionate about? There is something here for everyone. Learning a new skill or hobby can be a fun stress relieving activity, side hustle, way to stay in shape, and keep your creative juices flowing.

1. Adult coloring book
2. Baking
3. Calligraphy
4. Cooking
5. Crochet
6. DIY Project
7. Gardening
8. Invest
9. Learn a new language (sign, Spanish, Swahili etc.)
10. Learn to dance
11. Listen to Podcast
12. Musical Instrument
13. Photography
14. Scrapbooking
15. Sewing (embroidery)
16. Start a BLOG
17. Volunteer
18. Watch Documentaries
19. Write a book
20. Yoga

M

Meditation allows you to discover your true authentic self by quieting your mind and moving your body.

M – Meditate.

Meditation is one of the simplest, most powerful, most wonderful self-care strategies. It creates a sense of calm and inner harmony in a world that is, at times, busy and noisy. Meditation is a way to stop, be still, eliminate distractions, solve problems, be creative, and increase happiness. Research has shown that meditating improves the function of your brain and extends your lifespan. For example, mediation has been found to lower blood pressure, reduce anxiety, increase cardiovascular health, improve sleep, and reduce symptoms of depression. Meditation allows you a few minutes of inner peace. Just three to five minutes a day of meditation has proven health benefits. Start with short intervals of time and gradually increase the amount of time you spend slowing down, being still and in the moment as your comfort and confidence levels grow.

I like to meditate at the start of the day when it seems like the whole world is quiet. I also find it helpful to find a quiet place in the middle of the day at work to disconnect for a few minutes. Sometimes I set my phone alarm and just lay my head back and close my eyes for 10 minutes and just breathe. It is amazing what 10 minutes of peace in the middle of the workday can do for your mental stability. It gets more challenging for me to block out noise and distractions as the day progresses.

There are various meditations, such as mindfulness, spiritual, focused, movement, mantra, transcendental, progressive, loving-kindness, and visualization. Some are easily practiced alone, while others require a little more guidance. Practice the one that meets your needs and fits your unique personality and lifestyle.

Dr. Gwen's Self-Care Tip:

Set aside time each day and find a place where you can let your mind completely relax. Spend this time reconnecting with yourself. You are worthy. If needed, you can use an app to help you. Headspace.com and Calm.com are two that are popular and come highly recommended.

N

Saying yes is a responsibility.

Saying NO is a choice.

When you practice self-care, you answer with a fidelity that eliminates guilt and resentment.

N – "NO!" Say it, mean it and do not feel guilty about it.

It is okay to say a firm "NO" to colleagues or even supervisors when you are overloaded and overwhelmed. Saying no does not make you a negative or selfish person. Paulo Coehlo says, "When you say YES to others, make sure you are not saying NO to yourself." Saying no to things you are not passionate about means leaving room for saying yes to things you like or want to participate in. Do not feel guilty about saying no or think you owe others an elaborate explanation. Saying no frees up your time and allows you to focus on your own list of priorities. To be the most effective and efficient in your role, you need to focus on your priorities before saying yes to others. This might require you to say no to helping a colleague who often procrastinates and saying yes to that relaxing mani/pedi appointment or massage you planned weeks ago. Many times, you are coerced or "voluntold" to participate in events or projects simply because you cannot say no. If you want to start taking better care of yourself, you must learn to say no to tasks, invites, engagements, promotions, and opportunities that may not align with your short and long-term goals. Being a people pleaser can lead to doing things that you do not want to do, and do not have time for, which leads to resentment and inevitably burnout. When you say no, you allow others the opportunity to grow by allowing them to step up. In a sense, everyone wins.

Saying "NO" applies to friends and family as well. Remember, your needs matter too!

Dr. Gwen's Self-Care Tip:

Here are some "polite" ways to say no for those of you who have difficulty doing so. Hopefully, these suggestions will give you the confidence to make your needs a priority. I am rooting for you.

1. **The direct approach.**

   It leaves no room for false hope. NO really is a complete sentence. There is no need for further explanation.

   I'm sorry but I can't.

2. **It's not my decision.**

   My husband is notorious for using me as his scapegoat.

   Thanks so much for the invite, but I promised my wife I would .....

3. **Offer an alternative.**

   I cannot attend the event, but I will make a donation.

   I cannot attend, but I will spread the word.

   I can't but Sally really enjoys _____ so she might be interested.

4. **Try a little gratitude.**

   I appreciate you asking, but I will not be able to participate at this time.

   I appreciate you thinking of me, but I have a prior engagement.

5. **Be transparent**

   I have not been feeling my best lately, so I am not taking on anything else right now.

Use the lines below to prepare a few ways to say no. Think of reasons that are relevant to you and practice saying them to build your confidence.

_____

_____

_____

_____

_____

_____

O

Organizing and decluttering provides the opportunity to live in a useful space of beauty that brings you peace, joy, and sparks creativity.

O – Organize and declutter your work, home, and life.

Organizing and decluttering, simply stated, is a way to eliminate the unnecessary. It allows you to live a more productive and simplistic life. Focus and concentration are difficult to maintain when you are surrounded by clutter and excessive things. Think about trying to work at a messy, disorganized desk. It is virtually impossible to get anything accomplished when you are surrounded by mounds of papers. It can be incredibly stressful.

There are numerous benefits to organizing and decluttering your space, home, and ultimately your life. The benefits include:

- Reduces stress and anxiety by creating order.
- Makes cleaning the house easier.
- You may find hidden treasures.
- It allows you to enjoy the space.
- Eliminates shame and embarrassment.
- Improves your sleep.
- It rids your home of allergens (dust, pet hair, and pollen) that could make you sick (allergies, hay fever, asthma, eczema).
- Boost productivity and creativity.

Dr. Gwen's Self-Care Tip

Declutter your life of people and things that are pulling you away from productivity and peaceful living. There is a big, beautiful world free of stress and anxiety hiding behind the mounds of clutter and disorganization.

Here are a few tips to get you started.

1. **Create a decluttering checklist.** It is a lot easier to declutter your life if you have a plan. There are many examples of declutter checklist that can be found on the internet.

2. **Donate.** Give unused or unneeded items to Goodwill or the Salvation Army.

3. **Use the Box System**. Get three boxes and label them: keep, give away, or trash. Start with small spaces (office, kitchen, or bathroom drawer) and then move to larger spaces (pantry, closet, bedroom).

4. **Eliminate Duplicates**. How many old laptops do you have around the house? What about cellphones and chargers? TV's? Electronics? Curling Irons? Hair dryers? I am going to come right out and say it. Do not hesitate, or think twice about it, let all but one of your duplicate items go.

5. **Pay off debts**. Decluttering and living more simplistically will help you build up savings and get rid of those unwanted credit card debts.

6. **Reduce and Recycle.** Keep a small trash or recycling bin in each room to encourage the elimination of unneeded items right away.

7. **Store seasonal items**. Keep seasonal items (clothing, decorations, tools, etc.) stored away until needed in the closet, attic, storage shed, or under the bed.

8. **Label Items.** When things have a proper place and are labeled for easy access, there tends to be less clutter.

9. **Invest in Storage Options.** Buy some filing cabinets, plastic bins, and organizers to place everything currently in disarray.

10. **Computerize**. Computerize your receipts, bills, invoices, and other miscellaneous sheets of paper to save trees and space. Make sure you store information in an area that is backed up regularly.

11. **Watch Hoarding: Buried Alive on TLC**. Hoarding disorder is real. After watching an episode of this show, I am sure you will be motivated to get started. You may pick up a few additional decluttering tips too.

12. **Progress over perfection**. Focus on accomplishing small goals and keep chipping away at that declutter list. Acknowledge and celebrate your small wins.

P

The key is not to prioritize what's on your schedule, but to schedule your priorities.

~ Stephen Covey

P – Prioritize.

Greg Wells, best-selling author of *The Ripple Effect* and *Rest, Refocus, Recharge,* says we need to stop practicing time management and start practicing priority management. Priority management means deciding what is most important to you (dreams and goals) and allocating time to those tasks to decrease busyness, increase meaningful productivity, and improve health and relationships.

Action expresses priorities!

Dr. Gwen's Self-Care Tip

Prioritize your goals and take action.

1. Improve your health.

2. Strengthen relationships.

3. Go back to graduate school.

4. Dress for success.

5. Land that dream job.

6. Buy your dream car.

7. Buy your dream house.

8. Get out of debt.

9. Save for retirement.

10. Have FUN.

Q

Quit giving energy and attention to everything and everyone that weighs you down.

Q – Quit bad habits and things that are not working.

Today is a great day to stop doing that self-destructive thing you do. No more excuses!

According to Stephen Covey, you have more power than you think over the things that feel out of your control. Therefore, you can take responsibility for your work concerns and be more proactive, productive, and happier. I find that when sitting through webinars or VTC's at my desk, I am more engaged when I kick off my heels and walk in place as opposed to sitting at my desk and, in most cases, fighting to stay awake or snacking. You will be amazed at how many steps you can get in the span of thirty minutes to an hour.

As a counselor, you can better manage or control your workday schedule. You can start by scheduling time for lunch and breaks during the day. Take 10-15 minutes between clients to stretch, walk around the office/building, or simply rehydrate with water. Leave room in your schedule to decompress after a difficult client or meeting. Do not schedule demanding clients back-to-back who drain your energy.

Dr. Gwen's Self-Care Tip

Here are 25 things that are okay to quit. Quitting can be a virtue.

STOP...

1. Being a people pleaser.

2. Resisting change.

3. Living in the past.

4. Negative self-talk.

5. Smoking.

6. Being the victim.

7. Saying yes when you really want to say no.

8. Complaining.

9. Suffering in silence.

10. Overindulging,

11. Procrastinating.

12. Lying (to yourself and others).

13. Letting fear and doubt hold you back.

14. Doing the same thing and expecting different results (that's insane).

15. Praying everything is going to work itself out. (Faith without work is dead).

16. Eating unhealthily.

17. Cheating.

18. Being so hard on yourself.

19. Making excuses.

20. Being a control freak. Just let it go!

21. Being ungrateful.

22. Settling for less than you deserve.

23. Surrounding yourself with Debbie Downers.

24. Staying up late. Go to sleep!

25. Cutting corners. Do the right thing.

R

Each person deserves a day away in which no problems are confronted, no solutions searched for. Each of us needs to withdraw from cares which will not withdraw from us.

~ *Maya Angelou*

R – Rest and Re-energize.

Studies show that sleep and rest are essential building blocks of the body and mind, which are intrinsically connected. Proper rest allows your brain to repair, restore, rebuild, and regenerate. Your body and mind work so hard for you every day; treat it like your temple and give it time to replenish. Even your computer is programmed to sleep. When we spend all our time in hustle, bustle, and hustle some more mode and do not get adequate sleep, we increase our risk for cancer, cardiovascular disease, type 2 diabetes, and depression. We also increase the risk of burnout and exhaustion, which can lead to behavioral disorders and cognitive decline.

Taking time to rest and recuperate will do wonders for your life. Getting adequate sleep will recharge your ability and renew your energy and enthusiasm to deal with challenges at work, personal commitments, your relationships, and your overall health and well-being. When you build your energy reserves, you will be able to give from your surplus instead of trying to give from an empty cup. Rest is a worthy investment of your time because the reward is better productivity in every aspect of your life.

Dr. Gwen's Self-Care Tip:

Take "**Brain Breaks**" throughout the day. A brain break is a simple mental and/or physical activity that helps re-energize and re-engage the brain. Brain Breaks help to soothe the mind, settle fidgeting, minimize disruptive behavior, improve concentration, and reduce stress and anxiety. We could all benefit from taking brain breaks routinely or when the need arises to destress and manage our emotions. Check out Dr. Gwen's Brain Break Kit for kids at drgwenscounselorcafe.com/shop.

To fully rest and recharge, schedule brain breaks throughout the year. Do not settle for random downtime here and there. Educators, here is a little secret. You do not have to wait until spring or summer break when you are completely exhausted, mentally drained, and nearing burnout to take a vacation. That is the whole purpose of vacation days. When was the last time you took a vacation (GIRLS TRIP), a day to reconnect with a friend or family member, or a simple mental health day from work? If you are waiting on permission.... here you go.... APPROVED!

S

Setting boundaries and goals are healthy

normal

and necessary

even at the risk of

disappointing others.

S – Set boundaries and goals.

As educators (teachers and counselors), we often become attached to the students we serve and have difficulty forgetting about their problems at the end of the day. While developing meaningful relationships with students/clients is encouraged and expected, you should take steps to leave your job behind at the end of the day. When you bring your work home with you and continue to think about your students (parents, colleagues), it is hard to take time for yourself and even harder to focus on your own life (husband, kids, family, hobbies) outside of school. No matter how busy you are (and trust me, I know how busy you are), you will be far more efficient and effective in the long run if you leave your work at work. Do not worry. It will still be there tomorrow when you get back. Just pick up where you left off and keep pressing forward.

The American Institute of Stress ranks work-life balance as the top workplace stress area. When you leave work at the end of the day, make time to engage in activities you enjoy with your friends and loved ones. You and your partner or spouse might spend some time cooking a meal together, watching your favorite television shows, or simply going for an evening stroll. If you are not married or in a relationship, you can turn to your friends for help. An after-work dinner date or happy hour with friends may be just what the doctor ordered to get you attending to tasks that take your mind off work.

Dr. Gwen's Self-Care Tip:

Here are some examples of boundaries. Practice these and come up with some of your own.

Looks Like:
- Beginning and ending work on time.
- Reserving time in your schedule for a healthy lunch every day.
- Doing something you enjoy (ME TIME).
- Taking responsibility for your own happiness.
- Taking care of yourself (physically and emotionally).
- Setting and adhering to boundaries.

Sounds Like:

- No! Saying it without feeling guilty.
- Speaking up for yourself. It is okay to disagree.
- Thanks for the invitation but unfortunately, I will not be able to make it.
- I respect your opinion, but this is my decision.
- I do not respond to work emails after the duty day.
- I am not going to listen to you if you cannot match my tone.
- Asking for what you need (help, support, resources).

Feels Like:

- Confidence.
- Exhilaration.
- Freedom.
- Not being taken for granted.
- Strength.
- Support.
- Ownership.
- Safety.
- Satisfaction.

Write boundaries that you **WILL** set.

Family:

_____

_____

_____

_____

_____

Friends:

_____

_____

_____

_____

_____

Work:

_____

_____

_____

_____

_____

Home:

_____

_____

_____

_____

_____

T

TALK in such a way that others love to LISTEN to you.

LISTEN in such a way that others love to TALK to you.

T – Talk to a colleague or trusted friend.

Every good conversation starts with a good listener. Counselors, we got this! A good listener can connect with others on a deeper level and build deeper relationships. Designate someone you trust to be your echo chamber when things get too overwhelming and stressful. The opportunity to rant to someone for a few minutes during the day is worth its weight in gold. However, confidentiality is essential, so if there is not someone in your building you fully trust to keep confidences, choose someone off-site (friend, mentor, colleague, coach) who you can reach out to by phone. Remember, if you vent to someone about a student, parent, or colleague, honor confidentiality by not using names. Having a direct, assertive conversation is professional and effective.

Seek out people who have the right mindset, are passionate, engaged, positive, and supportive. These are the people who will lighten your load and vice versa.

Dr. Gwen's Self-Care Tip:

Call a supportive (friend, family member, colleague, mentor, coach) you have not spoken to lately.

Who did you call?

_____

_____

_____

_____

_____

What was your reaction to hearing the person's voice?

_____

_____

_____

_____

_____

What was their reaction to hearing your voice?

_____

_____

_____

_____

How long did the call last?

_____

_____

_____

_____

How did you feel after the call?

_____

_____

_____

_____

_____

What plans did you make to stay connected?

_____

_____

_____

_____

LISTENING is an art that REQUIRES

Attention over Talent

Spirit over Ego

Others over Self.

~ Dean Jackson

U

Unfollow anyone on social media and in life who does not make you feel

empowered

informed

or inspired.

U – Unfollow people who make you feel bad about yourself.

What you consume has a tremendous impact on your mindset and mental health. That is why it is important to routinely assess the media you consume and eliminate anything or anyone who conflicts with your well-being and personal or professional goals.

Social media has its pitfalls and benefits. If you are constantly exposed to images and stories of perfect lives, your mental health will be negatively affected. However, use social media in a controlled and limited way to share celebrations, congratulate each other, offer encouragement, or ask questions about what and how people are doing. It can be an inspiring form of connection. Use social media to create a community of support and build deeper, stronger, more meaningful relationships. It should not be used as a means of comparison between the life you live and small snapshots of others' lives.

Dr. Gwen's Self-Care Tip

You may have heard that we are the sum (money, fitness, and happiness) of the five people we spend the most time around. If you are spending an inordinate amount of time following someone online, they count too.

Write down the five people you spend the most time around. Then ask yourself are these people breathing life into you or sucking the life right out of you.

1.

2.

3.

4.

5.

Do not stop there. Assess your social self-care. Take some time to go through your apps, contacts, social media, podcasts, books, magazine subscriptions, and other information sources or connections and purge unhealthy influences. Remove (block, unfollow, unfriend, delete) anything and everything (family and friends included) that is not progressive or brings you joy. It is okay to love from a distance. You do not have to feel guilty or try to explain why you have prioritized your health and happiness. Remember your worth, and do not settle for the mundane. Surround yourself with people who elevate you and who you elevate in return. We rise by lifting others.

Who did you disconnect? What things did you let go? Why?

_____

_____

_____

_____

_____

_____

_____

_____

_____

_____

_____

_____

_____

V

The best way to find yourself is to lose yourself in the service of others.

~ *Mahatma Gandhi*

V – Volunteer in your community.

Volunteering brings hope and inspiration to others. It is gratifying work. Volunteers do not necessarily have the time; they just have the motivation, compassion, heart, and willingness. Get involved in an organization or grassroots group that you believe in. This is an opportunity to use your voice and talents for the common good and make the world a better place. We are all connected.

Research suggests that doing things for others is great for mental health, stress, and happiness. It is just what the doctor ordered to combat loneliness, which is a difficult emotion to self-soothe. You will be around others with common interests, interacting and making connections. People will show appreciation and give thanks for your time, service, and commitment. An added benefit is that you gain skills, experience, networking contacts, and build relationships that can potentially bolster your resume, make you more marketable, and turn you into a better human being.

Dr. Gwen's Self-Care Tip

If you find yourself with some extra time on your hands, it is good to give. Why not pay it forward and spread a little kindness and selflessness by volunteering. Consider committing a few hours to a worthy cause and pad that resume. Who knows, you may learn an entirely new set of talents that may change the trajectory of your career.

Here are some suggestions:

- Animal Shelters

- Churches

- Food Banks

- Habitat for Humanity

- Homeless Shelters

- Hospitals

- Libraries

- Museums

- Parks and Beaches

- Political Campaigns

- Red Cross

- Retired & Senior Programs

- Schools and Colleges

- Tutoring

- Youth Organizations

- Civic Organizations

Here are some questions to ask yourself as you consider when and where to volunteer.

1. What are my interests?

2. What are my skills?

3. What are some places in my community that match my interests and skills?

4. What do I hope to gain from the experience?

5. How many times do I want to volunteer (one time, short-term, on-going)?

6. Do I want to work alone or in a group?

7. Will I incur any expenses and if so, will I be reimbursed?

8. When can I start?

W

Drink more water....

Your skin

Your hair

Your mind and

Your body

will thank you.

W – Water; drink more of it.

Getting enough water daily is important for your health. Studies have shown that there is a link between water and stress reduction. All organs, including the brain, need water to function properly. Dehydration leads to a host of problems: headaches, fatigue, muscle weakness, and oxygen flow to the brain. It causes the heart to work harder to pump oxygen to all your organs, thereby making you more tired and less alert. By staying hydrated, you are better equipped to deal with daily challenges.

Hydration is an energy booster. You should drink a minimum of 8–10 cups (1 cup = 8 oz) per day but aim for 10–12 cups if you are more active. In general, you should try to drink between half an ounce to an ounce of water for every pound you weigh every day. For example, if you weigh 200 pounds, drink 100 to 200 ounces of water a day. Drink Up!

Dr. Gwen's Self-Care Tip

Choose water to boost your mood, improve brain and body functions, lose weight, and get a better night's rest.

There is a quote that says drinking water is like taking a shower on the inside of your body! Imagine that.

Here are 5 crafty ways to increase your water intake.

1. Flavoring your water with citrus fruits, like lemon and lime, can liven up your water. Fruits make water taste better and make it easier to consume for you reluctant water drinkers.

2. Eat your water. Most of the water we consume by drinking. However, you can get some fluids through the foods that you eat as well. For example, broth soups and foods with high water content such as fruits and vegetables can increase your daily intake.

3. Always keep water with you. You are more likely to drink it if you have it readily available. Keep a bottle/cup on your desk so it is a visible reminder and replace it throughout the day.

4. Order water when dining out. This will keep you hydrated, save money, and reduce calories all at the same time.

5. Keep a "water intake" journal. Setting a daily goal and monitoring your intake can help motivate you to maintain your fluid requirements. Try one of the many apps that track fluids, calories, and nutrients.

Here are recommended times studies have shown to maximize the benefits of drinking water.

- Drinking water in the morning when you first wake up will kick start your brain and internal organs.

- Drinking water before a meal helps with digestion and reduces caloric intake, especially in older adults.

- Drinking plenty of water before and after exercising helps you stay hydrated, replenishes vital fluids lost during your workout and supports recovery.

- Drinking a glass of water before a shower can help lower your blood pressure.

- Drinking a glass before bed helps to reduce the risk of stroke and heart attacks.

However, the most important thing is to drink water consistently throughout the day to stay hydrated.

X

When life hands you a Xylophone – live out loud!

X – Xylophone.

Here you are...after a rough day at work/school...you are on the drive home, you turn on the radio, and your jam just happens to come on. You know, the song that gets your head bobbing, fingers snapping, and body bouncing. You crank up the volume and start singing in blissful ignorance at the top of your lungs, releasing all the chaos and fatigue of the day. Instantly you get a boost of energy, and your mood improves. That's the magic of music.

Music is the soundtrack of our lives. We often forget how much music permeates so many aspects of our being. Certain songs can bring forth precious memories - your childhood, first dance, holidays, seasons, wedding day, etc.

Music has a way of evoking a range of emotions such as joy, sadness, and fear. It has been said that music touches you in places where words alone cannot. Music is a universal language that we all understand. Sometimes music is the only medicine the heart and soul need to heal wounds and remove sadness, fear, and doubt. According to some researchers, music has positive effects on physical and mental health and well-being. Music reduces stress and anxiety, improves our mood, and eases pain. Many hospitals and medical facilities use music therapy as part of a patient's treatment for medical, physical, emotional, and cognitive needs. Fifteen minutes a day is all you need to boost your mood, decrease stress, and improve sleep quality.

Here are some ways to incorporate music into your daily life. It is easy to do. Music can lift your mood, so put on some feel-good music if you feel sad and blue. Upbeat music can give you a boost of energy. For example, listening to music while doing daily chores make them less daunting, and you complete tasks more quickly. Combining music with an exercise such as walking, or aerobics can increase health benefits. A slower music tempo can relax your mind and body. It is a great way to reduce stress.

Dr. Gwen's Self-Care Tip

Create a self-care playlist. It could be a playlist of your favorite feel-good songs, a playlist of songs to help you relax and calm down, or a playlist for when you need a good soul-cleansing cry. I have provided space for two playlists, but you do not have to stop there. Create as many as you like.

Playlist Type:

Song/Artist:

1.

2.

3.

4.

5.

6.

7.

8.

9.

10.

Playlist Type:

Song/Artist:

1.

2.

3.

4.

5.

6.

7.

8.

9.

10.

One good thing about music, when it hits you, you feel no pain.

~ Bob Marley

Y

Yoga adds

energy

strength

and beauty

to your body, mind, and spirit.

~ *Amit Ray*

Y – Yoga provides physical and mental health benefits.

Yoga is a practice that emphasizes mind-body-energy connections for people of all ages. Research shows that yoga improves strength, balance, flexibility, back pain, arthritis symptoms, and heart health. According to the National Institutes of Health, scientific evidence shows that yoga supports stress management, mental health, mindfulness, healthy eating, weight loss, and sleep. It is one of the simplest exercises you can do to improve your health, mind, body, and spirit. Did I mention that it has been said that yoga increases your sex drive too? Hurry up, grab a yoga mat, some comfortable clothes, and strike a pose. Harvard Health Publications suggest the **Cobra Pose** for enhanced sexual function.

Dr. Gwen's Self-Care Tip

Here are a few popular yoga poses. Each of these poses has its own unique challenges and benefits and can be practiced in isolation or as part of a routine.

1. **Mountain Pose** helps improve balance, patience and brings your attention to the here and now.

2. **Downward Dog Pose** lengthens and decompresses the spine, stretches the hamstrings, strengthens your arms, hand, and wrist, flushes your brain with fresh oxygen, and calms your mind. It also reduces symptoms of menstruation and menopause, in addition to preventing osteoporosis.

3. **Child Pose** is a resting, restorative, and calming pose. It helps to relieve neck, back, and hip strain. It stretches the lower back and shoulders, opens the hips, and even helps fight insomnia. This pose also eases menstrual pain for women and lowers anxiety levels.

4. **Warrior I Pose** is a great pose to relax your body and mind after a stressful day. It strengthens your legs and opens your chest and shoulders, which helps with posture and mellows the mind.

5. **Warrior II Pose** like the Warrior I pose strengthens your legs and arms, opens your chest, and shoulders, and contracts your abdominal organs. It can also be therapeutic for sciatica and backaches.

6. **Triangle Pose** improves your spine's flexibility; it helps with the alignment of your shoulders; it relieves back pain and stiffness in the neck area.

7. **Squat Pose** helps strengthen the lower back, stretch the groin, tone the belly, and release tension in the hips and knees.

8. **Cat Cow Pose** improves posture and balance and strengthens and stretches the neck, arms, abdomen, and back.

9. **Butterfly Pose** is a simple stretch that stimulates blood circulation and relieves symptoms of menstruation and menopause.

10. **Corpse Pose** is one that many yoga classes end with. It rejuvenates your mind and body by relaxing you and relieving stress and fatigue. It shifts attention to your inner self while lowering your blood pressure, calming you, and giving your body the opportunity to absorb all the benefits of a good workout.

Participating in a yoga class is a great way for beginners to learn correct posturing and techniques. It is also a way to combat loneliness and participate in group healing and support.

Z

Live a more Zen-like life.

You cannot always control what happens to you but, you can always control how you respond.

Z – Zero tolerance for negative energy…. Zen!

One of my favorite words is simplify. For years I have kept a small wooden star on the desk in my office with the word "simplify" as a reminder. Think for a moment about the simplicity of a monk's life. I visited a monastery a few years ago and witnessed the concentration and mindfulness that Monks put into everyday activities such as cleaning, cooking, and gardening. There was such a sense of peacefulness and calm that seemed to radiate from them and the whole compound.

Like me, maybe one of your goals is to live a more Zen-like life, full of peace, tranquility, and joy. We can start by not letting our words and actions, or those from others, disturb, disrupt, or destroy our inner peace and dim our light. As educators, we are faced with challenges daily. The way we take our power back is how we respond to those challenges.

Dr. Gwen's Self-Care Tip

Here are a few ways to incorporate Zen-like practices into your daily life.

1. **Make Preparations the Night Before**

   A sure-fire way to get your day off to a hectic start is by running late because you overslept, could not decide what to wear, could not find your keys, did not have time for breakfast and did not pack a lunch.

   Your Zen-like day should start the night before. I write in a gratitude journal nightly. I give thanks for the day, but I also set goals and actions for the next day. This helps me to progress and stay focused.

   I also iron my clothes for the week and pick out accessories (undergarments, shoes, jewelry) at night to cut down on time in the morning.

   I decide what I am going to eat for breakfast and pack my healthy lunch and snacks the night before. This keeps me from skipping meals or filling my day with fast on the go foods.

2. **Morning Meditation**

   I have already written about meditation and the benefits previously (refer to letter M). Now here is an additional reason to meditate: to add Zen to your life. Starting your day with just a few minutes of meditation can set the tone for your whole day.

3. **Keep A Zen Attitude**

   A Zen attitude is knowing that challenges will come but that you have the power to conquer them all. Refer to letter C, where I discussed changing your mindset and attitude.

4. **Simply BE**

   When you are planning your schedule for the day, make your day more Zen by taking time to incorporate calming activities. Here are a few things you can do:

   - Blow bubbles.

   - Do 5-5-5 deep breathing (see letter B).

   - Go for a short walk.

   - Smile and think happy thoughts.

   - Soak up a few rays of sunshine.

   - Stretch.

   - Take brain breaks.

Afterwards

Congratulations on completing Dr. Gwen's A to Z Self-Care Guide. You did it! However, this is just the beginning of your self-care journey. Self-care is a life-long commitment. Keep making yourself a priority and doing the things that bring you joy and feed your soul. I am proud of the work you are doing. You should be too!

I enjoyed writing this book. I made sure to hit every aspect of self-care to include physical, emotional, psychological, spiritual, and professional. There is something here for everyone, no matter what area of self-care you need to improve. We are always learning and growing, and our lives are constantly changing. One day, month, or year you may need to focus on one area of self-care, and tomorrow, next month, or next year your needs may change. That is okay. Adjust and make changes as needed.

Now that you have journeyed from A to Z, I encourage you to add to the list. There is so much more that self-care could cover for each letter. For example, J for join a group. K for Kindness. S for Smile. I am curious to know what you would have chosen for each letter. Feedback is information that can help us grow. It also provides information for others to begin their self-care journey. Visit Dr. Gwen's Counselor Café on Facebook, Instagram, or send me a private email at drgwencounselorcafe.com with feedback. I would appreciate it if you would leave a review on Amazon or on my website, drgwenscounselorcafe.com. You will also find additional helpful resources on the website, such as my blog, where I share even more useful tips, and a shop where self-care items can be purchased.

Peace and Blessings,

Dr. Gwen

SELF-CARE REFLECTIONS

AWARENESS, GROWTH, GOALS

This is an opportunity for you to write what you learned about yourself, growth opportunities and future goals.

_____

_____

_____

_____

_____

_____

_____

_____

_____

_____

_____

_____

_____

_____

_____

_____

Keep Going

Whether you are an avid self-care enthusiast or just now committing to taking the first steps on this journey to becoming healthier, and happier, share your progress and inspire your friends and family to do the same.

Maintain a growth mindset so that you will continue to be a life-long learner. Self-care is an on-going commitment to being the absolute best YOU! Take the information and tips that you learned from this A to Z Guide and apply them to every aspect of your life. Commit to being just a little bit better each day. Remember small consistent changes and time yield BIG results.

It does not matter how slowly you go as long as you do not stop.

~ Confucius

Difficult roads lead to beautiful destinations.

My Commitment

Make a commitment to yourself on how you will continue your self-care journey. As previously discussed, writing it down and sharing it with someone will make it more achievable and you more accountable. Then, take the self-care pledge.

_____

_____

_____

_____

_____

_____

_____

_____

_____

_____

_____

_____

Educator Self-Care Pledge

I, _____, am a dedicated Educator, and I promise to make self-care a top priority. I pledge to cultivate habits that honor ME, reduce stress, and enhance my overall health and well-being. I will take time each day to invest in ME, mind, body, and soul because I am worth it. My needs matter too!

Signed _____

Let's Stay Connected

I am so honored that you joined me on this self-care journey to better health and wellness. I hope this A to Z guide has been helpful, and you acquired useful tips, tools, and strategies along the way.

While you are here, take a minute to follow me on Facebook, Instagram, and YouTube for additional self-care tips, tools, strategies, and challenges. Connect with me on LinkedIn too. I would love to hear how you are utilizing the book and where you are on your self-care journey.

Join the Facebook Saving Ourselves Support Group (facebook.com/groups/154955292586988) to stay inspired and to inspire others.

You can find self-care products and resources, including my blog and books, at drgwenscounselorcafe.com.

 @drgwenscounselorcafe

 @drgwenscounselorcafe

 linkedin.com/in/drgwenscafe/

 Dr. Gwen's Counselor 's Cafe

Resources

Here are some resources that I find helpful and you may find helpful too, on this self-care journey to better health and wellness.

Apps

Action for Happiness
Calm.com
Down Dog
Headspace.com
Podcast
YouTube

Books

Autobiographies
Bible
Eat, Pray, Love
Leaving It at the Office
Mindset
Rest, Recharge, Refocus
The Ripple Effect
The Power of Positive Thinking
You Are A Badass

Places

Beach
Church
Conference
Garden
Gym
Museum
Nature
Park
Support Group
Vacation Destination

Music

Happy
He Saw the Best In Me
How Great Is Our God?
Just Fine
Lean on Me
Man in the Mirror
Roar
Stand
Stronger

Acknowledgements

For me, family is huge. I am grateful for my husband Carl who provides daily inspiration and encouragement. I am so lucky to have you as a life partner.

To my parents, thank you for your never-ending love and support. Dad you are my biggest champion and mom you are my prayer warrior. To Ms. Betty Joe, thanks for being the best mother-in-law a girl could hope for. You always believed I could do anything, and I NOW believe it too.

My friends are the family I choose to let into my inner circle. Special thanks to Marchell, Naz, and Jean, for providing a listening ear and pushing me to complete this project. Despite how much each of you have going on, you always take time to listen to all the ideas I have rolling around in this head of mine. Anyone who knows me knows that I am a talker, so your generosity has not gone unnoticed.

Thank you to my group members (Saving Ourselves Self-Care Group) for providing the motivation and creativity to come up with challenges to keep us moving in the right direction. Dr. Gwen's weekly self-care tips, tools and strategies videos began as a suggestion from one of you. You inspire me.

Finally, thank you to all the counselors and teachers (educators) who have allowed me to walk alongside you as we strive to take care of ourselves while giving care to others. We are bigger, better, stronger together! Twenty-three years ago, I became an educator. Between then and now, I got married, obtained four degrees, worked as a Special Education Teacher, Licensed Professional Counselor, College Professor, and embarked upon my own personal self-care journey. Through the years, creating content and materials that empower others to overcome challenges has been my greatest passion.

♡ ~ Notes ~ ♡

_____

_____

_____

_____

_____

_____

_____

_____

_____

_____

_____

_____

_____

_____

_____

_____

_____

_____

_____

♡ ~ Notes ~ ♡

♡ ~ Notes ~ ♡

♡ ~ Notes ~ ♡

Dr. Gwen's Counselor Cafe

Additional Self-Care Products

drgwenscounselorcafe.com/shop

Meet Dr. Gwen

Gwendolyn Martin, who goes by the name Dr. Gwen is a licensed professional counselor, educator (special education teacher, school counselor, professor), and advocate who is dedicated to spotlighting the importance of self-care in managing stress and cultivating health and happiness. She is the owner of Dr. Gwen's Counselor Café, a platform that provides effective self-care solutions for educators, including teachers, counselors, licensed clinicians, and other helping professionals. Her self-care products, group, workshops, speaking engagements, mentoring, consultation, and books help people transform their personal and professional lives. When she isn't working, she invests in self-care by spending time with her loved ones, nurturing her garden, cooking healthy vegetarian/pescatarian dishes, and cuddling up with a good romance novel. You can find out more about Dr. Gwen at drgwenscounselorcafe.com.

Made in United States
North Haven, CT
10 November 2021